IMAGES
of America

GHOSTS AND MURDERS OF MANHATTAN

Manhattan's nightscape is seen here from the haunted Empire State Building in 1937. The author invites you to journey down the dark streets of Manhattan's past and shine a light on its rich tapestry of people and places. (Courtesy of the Library of Congress.)

ON THE COVER: Built in 1877 as a courthouse, the Jefferson Market continues to be the touchstone of Greenwich Village. Today, it is a branch of the New York Public Library, and visitors can peruse periodicals in the basement where notorious criminals were held while awaiting trial or find a book in the former courtrooms on the first and second floors. For more information, see page 102. (Author's collection.)

IMAGES
of America

GHOSTS AND
MURDERS
OF MANHATTAN

Elise Gainer

ARCADIA
PUBLISHING

Published by Arcadia Publishing
Charleston, South Carolina

Printed in the United States of America

Library of Congress Control Number: 2013930467

For all general information, please contact Arcadia Publishing:
Telephone 843-853-2070
Fax 843-853-0044
E-mail sales@arcadiapublishing.com
For customer service and orders:
Toll-Free 1-888-313-2665

Visit us on the Internet at www.arcadiapublishing.com

To those gone but not forgotten

CONTENTS

ACKNOWLEDGMENTS

I gratefully acknowledge and give thanks to the staff at the Library of Congress, especially Jeff Bridges, Ellen Kays, and Marilyn Ibach, for assisting in unearthing jewels from their rich image archives. I also want to thank the staff in the copyright office for unraveling the tangled web of copyright restrictions.

I am indebted to the many historians and authors who investigated and wrote about some of the tales retold here. The bibliography, on page 127, offers this source information.

One of the greatest gifts that came out of researching this book was meeting my new friends from the Merchant's House Museum, including Anthony Bellov, Margaret Halsey Gardiner, and Tina Cuadrado. I thank them for generously sharing their stories, images, and time. I look forward to reveling in the museum's magic in the years to come.

Some projects do not get started without a swift kick in the butt, so my thanks go to James Abel for motivating me to say "yes," and a special thank you is reserved for my editor, Rémy Louis Thurston, for asking me to do this in the first place.

I also appreciate the help from Brandon D'Orlando and JJ Ignotz as well all of the cheers from my family, friends, and coworkers.

Finally, this book would not have been possible without Jenny Yoo's unprecedented understanding and Ralph Herdman's editing, encouragement, and love.

Unless otherwise noted, images are courtesy of the Library of Congress, specifically their collections of George Grantham Bain, the Detroit Publishing Company, the *New York World-Telegram* and *Sun* Newspaper Photograph Collection, the National Photograph Company, the Farm Security Administration, Gottscho-Schleisner, the Historic American Buildings Survey, Van Vechten, Popular Graphic Arts, Stereograph Cards, and the US Geography File.

INTRODUCTION

The New Amsterdam Theatre audience emerged from the sunny make-believe world of Africa to find billowing snow blanketing Times Square. They bent into the wind, rushing to beat the brunt of the storm. In classic the-show-must-go-on spirit, the Disney Theatrical Group decided not to cancel the next day's matinee. Knowing it would be difficult for the cast and crew to travel to and from the show in the blizzard, they arranged for a slumber party at the theater.

After raiding the soda machine and munching on popcorn, ushers, actors, and wardrobe staff set up their cots in the ornate alcove behind the velvet, orchestra-level seats. A hardy young man from Brooklyn ventured out on his own. Using child booster cushions, he made a comfortable bed on a cozy landing in the back stairwell between the balcony and the main floor. Pleased with the privacy and quiet, he pulled his cap down over his eyes to block out the soft glow cast by the stairwell footlights. The heavy hammer of sleep had not yet fallen before the sound of distant footsteps awakened him. He listened for a moment, and, deciding it must be children from the cast playing around, he dozed off.

Hours passed and footfalls again roused him from sleep. The thuds grew louder as they descended from the balcony and stopped on the landing above his bed. He peered up the stairs but nothing shown in the small flood of light. When the darkness beyond did not answer back, he scolded his imagination and fell asleep again. Soon after dawn, urgent, heavy feet pounded up the stairs from the orchestra level, and as they reached his bed, he bolted up to avoid being trampled. Finding no one to confront, the young man failed to understand what had occurred. Olive Thomas, the long-dead follies star, flashed into his mind, wearing the fur-trimmed cloak she wore in the photograph in the lobby. Had she tried to get his attention? He had heard that she haunted the theater, but he shoved the thought from his mind, choosing instead the comfortable subjects of coffee and breakfast.

Ghost encounters like this point to the possibility that life continues after death. History chronicles what life once was, while murders remind us of the frailty that life is, and each is shrouded in mystery. To make sense of the apparitions seen at the Merchant's House Museum, to know what it was like to be imprisoned in the Sugar House during the Revolutionary War, or to comprehend what led John C. Colt to bludgeon to death a business associate is to grasp at smoke.

By combining historical images with stories of ghosts and murders, this book hopes to bring the reader closer to the subject. For those interested in the paranormal, the images set the stage and bring the characters into visual focus. For the historian, the stories add texture to the images by coloring the faces, buildings, and streets with human emotion and experiences.

Most of the stories are grouped by where they occurred. Hauntings associated with Washington Square Park, the Empire State Building, Grand Central Station, the Brooklyn Bridge, and others are in the first chapter, "Deadly Places, Public Spaces," along with the murderous events that happened on Wall Street and in Union Square, Five Points, and Hell's Kitchen.

The chapter "Lively Hotels and Homes" includes ghost stories about the Algonquin Hotel, the Hotel Chelsea, Gracie Mansion, the Morris-Jumel Mansion, the Dakota apartments, and activities on Gay, Tenth, and Bank Streets.

"Churches, Museums, and Mysterious Institutions" focuses on the paranormal activities in the graveyards of Trinity Wall Street, St. Mark's Church, St. Paul's Chapel, and St. Patrick's Old Cathedral. This chapter also relates numerous experiences at the Merchant's House Museum and the reasons why ghosts are associated with the Frick Collection and the Astor and Morgan Libraries. Deadly events at Bridewell's Prison and the Tombs are also covered.

Manhattan's most notorious and recognizable residents have their own chapter. "The Famous and the Infamous" discusses the inspector who botched the investigation of a purported Jack the Ripper slaying, the man suspected of being the real Boston Strangler, and the characters involved in the so-called Crime of the Century as well as the murder that captivated Edgar Allen Poe to the point that police considered him a suspect. Accounts of Prohibition-era gangsters and the first American policeman to be sentenced to death round out the section.

The final chapter, "Spirited Taverns and Theaters," opens and closes with two drinking establishments, made famous by Dylan Thomas and George Washington, respectively. The ghosts of Broadway's grand theaters—the Palace, New Amsterdam, the Richard Rogers, and the Belasco—combine with the tragedies at the Metropolitan Opera House and the Astor Place riots to complete the book.

Hopefully, this dark journey will illuminate some of Manhattan's mysteries.

One

DEADLY PLACES,

PUBLIC SPACES

When the Social Conference of Unemployed scheduled a demonstration on March 28, 1908, at 2:00 p.m. in Union Square, the parks bureau denied their request for a permit to speak. The huge crowd that gathered found a large police presence and the area roped off. This must have angered the self-professed radical socialist Selig Cohen, who called himself Selig Silverstein, for he returned to the square at 3:30 p.m. with a bomb.

As Silverstein approached a cluster of police near the park's center fountain, he nervously lit a cigarette and attempted to ignite the fuse to his bomb. Instead, he dropped the cigarette into the opening of the brass bulb containing nitroglycerine and dynamite. Sparks ignited, followed by a massive boom that shook people in the surrounding blocks. The bomb exploded in Silverstein's hand, and an innocent tailor next to him died. After a moment of stunned silence, chaos erupted, with people running in all directions. Police drove people from the square with their clubs and horses. A quick-thinking policeman attached a tourniquet to Silverstein's arm and rushed him to the hospital, where Silverstein said he was sorry he had not killed any policemen. He died a month later after having his hand amputated.

Washington Square Arch marks the Fifth Avenue entrance to the haunted Washington Square Park. This arch, dedicated in 1895 and designed by Stanford White, replaced a temporary wooden structure built to commemorate the 100th anniversary of George Washington's inauguration as the first president. Minetta Brook once flowed diagonally from the north to the southwest corner, and the Native American Sapokanikan tribe used the land in the surrounding area as a burial ground. In 1797, the land officially became designated as a potter's field and, in the years following, as a place for public executions by hanging. Stories abound that on stormy nights the apparitions of bodies have been seen hanging from the trees. During the height of the dreaded yellow fever outbreaks, from 1791 to 1821, officials used the land for shallow mass graves. When the area was used as a parade ground in 1826, cannon wheels unearthed human remains, so, in 1827, a public park was established. An estimated 20,000 people were buried beneath the tree-lined pathways and monuments, which may explain why many visitors capture orbs in their photographs.

11

Since the opening of Central Park in 1857, New Yorkers have flocked to its treed paths, lush lawns, and placid waterways to escape the frenetic pace of the city. At times, danger has followed. Although never as sinister as it was often portrayed, the park did report 35 murders between 1979 and 1986. The most sensational murder of that era occurred on August 26, 1986, when an 18-year-old woman died by strangulation at the hands of Robert Emmet Chambers Jr. The victim had met Chambers while drinking at a bar the night before, and the newspapers dubbed the crime "the Preppie Murder." After a controversial trial, Chambers accepted a plea deal of manslaughter in the first degree and was sentenced to 5 to 15 years in prison. Released on February 14, 2003, Chambers found himself behind bars again in 2008, serving a 19-year sentence for selling drugs.

Historically, crime and tragedy are rare in Central Park. Since the Gilded Age, people have enjoyed rowing in the summer and skating in the winter. And before there were ice rinks, people glided across the frozen lake at Seventy-second Street. Irving Brokaw, seen here skating with his wife, Lucile, on the lake in 1913, was the first American to compete in the Winter Olympics, finishing in sixth place in 1908.

Two sisters' passion for ice-skating continues today. In the 1800s, Janet Van der Voort and her sister Rosetta lived unremarkable lives together, never marrying but skating often. Janet wore dark purple velvet, and Rosetta shined in a red velvet cutaway coat. Through the years, on crisp winter days and even on balmy summer ones, people have continued to see them floating just above the lake. The phantoms' antique costumes leave no doubt as to their identities.

According to New York City ghost experts, apparitions often mingle with visitors at Grand Central Terminal. Cornelius Vanderbilt orchestrated the construction of the Grand Central depot (above), which opened in 1871. On January 8, 1902, a New Haven & Hartford Railroad train bound for Grand Central waited on the tracks in the Park Avenue tunnel when a steam locomotive from the New York Central Railroad plowed into it. People sitting in the rear car were pinned against the hot boiler for up to two hours. Scores were injured, and the death toll rested at 17. Although the train's engineer proved to be at fault, the accident further spurred the movement for electric trains, so the New York Central Railroad board improved the Park Avenue tunnel and built a new station (left). Completed in 1913, the new terminal became the largest station in the world.

The waiting room, seen here in 1904, was demolished and replaced with the spacious Vanderbilt Hall. In 1913, witnesses described seeing an anxious man wandering the station, wringing his hands, and saying that the train to hell was coming for him at midnight. As 12:00 midnight struck, the man vanished, and in the distance, a whistle was heard, even though the next train was not due until 12:05 a.m.

The station faced demolition in 1968, but the city protected it by giving it landmark status. In 1990, the Metropolitan Transportation Authority accepted a $425-million plan for renovation. Today, an estimated 21 million visitors pass through its corridors yearly, not counting the dead ones. Some have seen an apparition of a man with a black mustache wearing a black suit in the balcony area, watching the crowd below.

When it was completed, the Brooklyn Bridge earned the distinction of being the longest steel suspension bridge in the world, yet tragedy marred its beginnings. In addition to the more than 30 deaths during construction, a dramatic event occurred on the first day the bridge opened to the public, Decoration Day, May 30, 1883. On that day, a woman's scream started a panic that resulted in 12 people being trampled to death in a stairway.

Suicide also casts a dark shadow on the bridge's beauty. Since it was opened, people have traveled from miles away to jump from its high girders. One Brooklyn policeman assigned to the night shift answered numerous reports of jumpers. On many occasions, he rushed to the bridge hoping to avert a tragedy, only to discover that witnesses were seeing the apparition of a man who had successfully committed suicide. The officer asked for a transfer.

The streets turned deadly on July 13, 1865, when the worst case of urban violence in the nation's history erupted after the government instituted a draft by lottery drawing. Anger boiled over on the day of the drawing, when the poor immigrant population learned that, for $300, an individual could buy an exemption from the draft. Mobs first looted and burned Republican-owned businesses, but as the madness intensified, the protestors began attacking the black community. Blaming African Americans for the war and for taking jobs, the rioters burned and hung many from trees. As a mob marched to the Colored Orphan Asylum on Fifth Avenue, adults whisked the children to a boat bound for Blackwell's Island (now Roosevelt Island). The riots lasted for three days until the government pulled troops off the front lines and sent them into the city.

THE RIOTERS BURNING THE COLORED ORPHAN ASYLUM, CORNER OF FIFTH AVENUE AND FORTY-SIXTH STREET, NEW YORK CITY.

THE FIVE POINTS IN 1859
View taken from the Corner of Worth & Little Water St

In 1808, the city filled in the sewage- and garbage-infested Collect Pond, a body of water north of Chambers Street. Three streets—Orange, Cross, and Anthony Streets—converged there, creating what became known as Five Points, seen here. The picturesque Paradise Square jutted into the intersection from the west. Unfortunately, because of poor engineering, the soft fill undermined foundations in the area, and poor drainage caused foul methane gas to escape. Affluent residents then left the area to poor immigrants and former slaves. On Cross Street, the Old Brewery, which once made Coutler's Beer, became an overcrowded tenement building, and the area around it earned the name Murderer's Alley. Although history does not support the legend that a murder a day occurred in Five Points, there is no disputing that the area stank, brothels abounded, and gangs ruled.

People crowded into the shabby tenement buildings in Baxter Alley, off Mulberry Bend east of Five Points. Jacob Riis took this photograph in 1888 and described the neighborhood as reeking with incest and murder. The violent Mulberry Boys, later named the Dead Rabbits, claimed the area as their territory. A political instrument of Tammany Hall, the Rabbits dictated how the neighborhood voted in elections.

In the 1880s, Mulberry Street became home to Italian immigrants and later powerful organized crime families. The Genovese, Bonanno, Gambino, and Gotti families had headquarters or owned establishments on the street. At 129 Mulberry Street, at the original location of Umberto's Clam House, a gunman shot dead the former Columbo mobster Joseph "Crazy Joe" Gallo while he dined with his family late on the night of April 6, 1972.

Pell and Mott Streets became the home of Chinese immigrants after railroad jobs dried up. Because they had no rights under the Chinese Exclusion Act, the mostly male population turned to traditional organizations known as tongs for support. Although most were legitimate operations, some dealt in gambling and drug dealing. Between 1900 and 1922, a total of 10 rival members from the Hip Sing Tong and the Four Brothers Society were murdered at numbers 9, 12, 21, 30 1/2, and 32 Pell Street (left). The On Leong Tong, another powerful Chinese organization with a violent past, had their headquarters at 14 Mott Street. On April 10, 1910, one of their gunmen allegedly started a shooting spree in front of 5 Mott Street (below). The ensuing battle between the Four Brothers, the Hip Song Tongs, and the On Leong Tongs lasted for four hours and killed four men.

Like Broadway, the Bowery began as a thoroughfare for the Native American population. It later became the road to Boston and a thriving theater district. After the elevated railroad arrived, sleazy bars and flophouses dominated the street. One notorious joint known as Suicide Hall stood at number 295. Legends abound that waiters robbed patrons and the downtrodden came there to end their lives. One Suicide Hall regular, Annie Moore, a known prostitute, lost her life at her ragged apartment a few blocks from the bar, in what the newspapers described as a "Ripper" murder. The man she lived with discovered her body on August 27, 1906. The killer slashed her throat and mutilated her body. Afterwards, an educated but tattered-looking man whom the locals called "Old Scratch" expressed a curious knowledge of Annie Moore's wounds and then disappeared. Moore's murder was never solved.

John Pierpont "Jack" Morgan Jr., born on September 7, 1867, followed his father's path into banking and philanthropy. He financed many of the Allied nations during World War I, angering some extremists, and on July 3, 1915, he suffered an assassination attempt at his Long Island mansion. He survived bullet wounds to his abdomen and hip, only to be the target of another mad person on September 16, 1920.

In this incident, the Trinity Church bells chimed the noon hour as a man drove a red wagon pulled by a bay-colored horse down Wall Street and stopped in front of the limestone-faced Morgan Building at Wall and Broad Streets. The driver threw the reigns over the back of the horse and disappeared. As the last bell struck, the horse and wagon vanished in a mushroom cloud of yellow and green smoke.

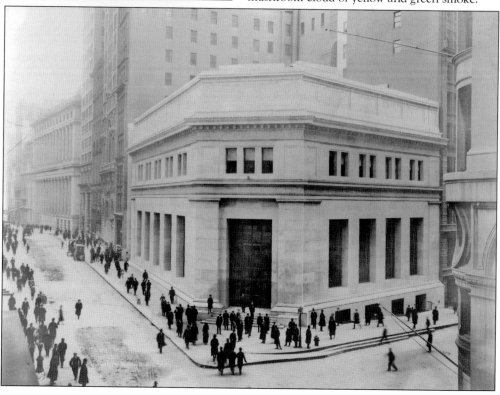

Witnesses described feeling a concussive force that blew some of them from their feet and sent a car into the side of the Morgan Building. Then came a roar, followed by a hushed silence that lasted until screams of agony filled the air. Shattered windows rained from surrounding skyscrapers. Flames licked through the broken openings, singeing the clothes of people cut by shards of glass. One chauffeur bending over to crank the engine of his vehicle found himself under the car a moment later, while his female passenger landed outside on the sidewalk. In a state of panic, injured people ran down to Beaver Street and up to Liberty Street, trailing blood behind them.

Disfigured bodies lay in pools of blood on the steps of the Morgan Building and across the street. More lay around the corner on Broad Street and up Wall Street toward Trinity Church. The force of the explosion decapitated one woman and blew the clothing off others. The dead and dying numbered 38, and more than 150 suffered injuries.

The Morgan Building, thought to be the target of the blast, sustained the most destruction. Despite the fact that the structure had been deemed sound, the offices inside were wrecked. Desks and chairs were overturned, and all lighting fixtures and windows broken. Remarkably, only one 28-year-old clerk died there, after being buried by a falling skylight. Jack Pierpont Morgan Jr. was away on holiday in England at the time of the attack.

According to the *New York Tribune*, this photograph was taken 10 minutes after the Wall Street explosion, as the surrounding structures emptied of people. Police rushed to the site and were later praised for their quick response despite being overworked from a recent transit strike. On the steps of what was then the sub-treasury, the unscathed statue of the nation's iconic leader, George Washington, seemed to grimly survey the death and destruction beyond his outstretched arm.

The blast sent an axle onto the 38th floor of an adjacent building. The mangled horse and wounds to the dead revealed that the bomber used cast-iron slugs from window sashes as projectiles. No one ever stood trial for the senseless murders, however, many years later, Italian anarchist Mario Buda became a popular suspect because of his known use of slugs as shrapnel in bombs.

Night watchman William Hoey was convicted of shooting to death patrolman Daniel Neville on August 27, 1921, in this lot at Thirty-ninth Street between Tenth and Eleventh Avenues. Violence reigned in the area between Thirty-fourth and Fifty-ninth Streets from Eighth Avenue to the Hudson River after the arrival of the Eleventh Avenue railroad in 1851. Warehouses, slaughterhouses, and shabby tenements crowded the area, which was populated by poor Irish and African Americans, who fought often. One legend on the origin of the neighborhood's name tells of two policemen watching a street fight on a hot August night with one noting, "This neighborhood is hot as hell." To this, his partner replied, "Hell's cool. This here is Hell's Kitchen." During those rough times, police always patrolled in pairs and only during daylight hours. The area became gentrified in the 1980s, and many celebrities moved in to be near the theater district.

On August 29, 1959, life imitated art. Two years after *Westside Story* opened on Broadway, gang violence visited this playground at Forty-sixth Street between Ninth and Tenth Avenues. A group of Puerto Rican teenagers calling themselves the Vampires planned to meet with an allied gang here at midnight. When they arrived and found boys they did not know, war chief Salvador Agrón stabbed Robert Young, who made it to the light-colored building at 449 West Forty-sixth Street before dying. Anthony Krzesinski sustained chest and groin wounds from Agrón and died in the hallway of number 447. Convicted of the murders, Agrón became the youngest man to sit on death row, at age 17. Gov. Nelson Rockefeller commuted Agrón's sentence days before his execution in 1962. He was released on parole in 1979 and died at the age of 43 in 1986.

This window adjacent to Police Plaza memorializes one of the deadliest buildings during the Revolutionary War, the Rhinelander Sugar House. Some historians claimed it had been turned into a British prison, where captured soldiers died from exposure, starvation, and disease. It is estimated that more people died in British prisons during the war than on the battlefield. For 100 years following the conflict, the Rhinelander building, once located at Rose (now William) and Duane Streets, had the reputation of being the most haunted site in the city. People heard moans and saw shadows at the windows and arms reaching through the bars. A new building replaced the old one in 1892, and when an original window from the prison was incorporated into the structure, ghostly activities continued in that area. In 1968, the city built the headquarters of the New York Police Department on the site, and the prison window was moved into the side of an obscure structure south of the plaza, perhaps to avoid further ghostly manifestations.

The Asch Building, at the intersection of Washington Place and Greene Street, housed the Triangle Shirtwaist Factory on its top three floors in 1911. Most of the employees were young immigrant women. Moods ran high on March 25, 1911, because quitting time came sooner on Saturdays. On the eighth floor at 4:40 p.m., as employees gathered their coats and belongings, supervisors started to pass out paychecks, and someone threw a cigarette butt into one of the bins. The tissue paper and scrap fabric burst into a ball of fire. People grabbed buckets of water that were on hand as required, but the materials were too flammable, rendering the water useless. The flames quickly engulfed the main exit area, so people ran to the rear exit, but workers had to wait for a manager to come and unlock the door. Brave elevator operators made as many trips as possible until the fire blocked their way. Someone called the operator on the 10th floor, and she alerted executives but never returned to her switchboard, so no one could then call the ninth-floor sewers.

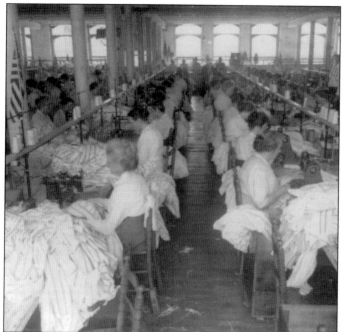

The sewers worked in a room that encompassed the Asch Building's entire ninth floor, similar to the Troy, New York, factory seen here. Machines hummed until 4:45 p.m., when the quitting bell sounded right as the fire reached them. Flame and smoke blocked the main entrance, so people rushed to the other staircase, but they found the exit door locked. No one had a key.

A group started down the fire escape located in the airshaft. Fire danced up from the eighth floor, making it a harrowing journey down. Abe Gordon, a button puncher, stepped through a broken window on the sixth-floor, and as he pulled his foot off the balcony, his clothes smoking, he heard a grinding screech followed by shrill screams as the fire escape collapsed, sending 24 souls to their death.

Firemen arrived at 4:47 p.m. to see bodies crashing to the pavement. They looked up to see faces pressed against the ninth-floor windows with flames behind them. The firemen extended their ladder to the sky, but it could only reach the sixth floor, 30 feet too short. They held out catch blankets for the jumpers, but the force of the fall ripped the blankets from the rescuers hands, and most victims died on impact.

On the Washington Place side of the building, one woman leaned out of a window and tossed her hat into the air. She opened her purse and dumped her money onto the crowd below. *United Press* reporter William Shepherd described how one man helped women onto the ledge and dropped them gently to the ground, writing that it was "as if he were helping them into a streetcar instead of into eternity."

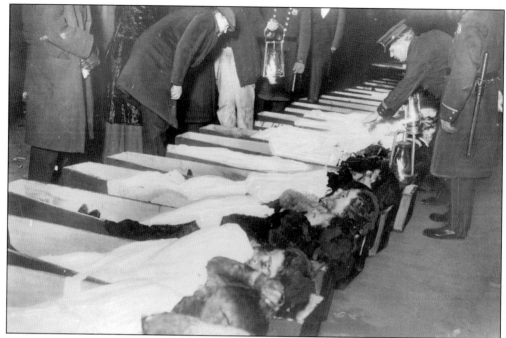

The last body fell from the Asch Building at 4:57 p.m. Just 17 minutes after the fire began, 146 people were dead or dying. Most were young women between the ages of 16 and 23. Authorities established a morgue on the pier at East Twenty-sixth Street, opening the doors to the public at midnight. Through the night, wails of grief echoed in the cavernous space, as more than 6,000 people per hour wandered what was termed Misery Lane.

The Asch Building, now the Brown Building, still stands and has a history of hauntings. On the ninth floor, people have heard a woman cry out in a foreign language. Some have seen apparitions of women running down the hallways, and still others have seen apparitions of the dead lying in the street. Also, many people have described a feeling of oppression upon entering the ninth floor.

Until the September 11, 2001, terrorist attacks on the World Trade Center, the Triangle Shirtwaist Factory fire was the deadliest workplace disaster in New York's history. Although the evidence indicated that supervisors locked the workers in, the factory owners, Max Blanck and Isaac Harris, were found not guilty of manslaughter. Later, they lost a civil suit and were ordered to pay $75 per victim. The victims did not die in vain, however, as this event shaped the future of the city. No longer could workers be locked in their workplace, fire equipment and codes changed, and worker's unions grew in power. Every year on March 25, the city's unions pay their respects at the intersection of Washington Place and Greene Street with fire trucks arriving and shooting their ladders to the sky to show that people will never forget.

Opened on May 1, 1931, the Empire State Building defied building standards. The tallest building in the world at the time, it was completed $5 million under budget and 45 days early. Made famous by the movie *King Kong* in 1932, it suffered a real-life tragedy on July 28, 1945, when a faulty B-25 plane crashed into the 79th floor. The pilot's wife, Martha Molloy Smith, suffered a premonition of disaster as her husband's plane lifted into the sky. A total of 14 people died in the crash; however, they are not the ghosts that haunt the tower. Instead, past suicides seem to generate the most unsettling experiences. Some have seen a woman appear on the observation deck attired in 1940s-period clothing, her lips painted red. Startled witnesses have reported her muttering about the death of her fiancé in Germany and then throwing herself over the barrier.

Two

LIVELY HOTELS
AND HOMES

The landmark Algonquin Hotel opened in 1902 and soon became a gathering place for artists, actors, and writers. Famous balladeers Harry Connick Jr., Diana Krall, and Michael Feinstein, among others, have entertained there. Behind bay windows, Orson Wells honeymooned, and Alan Jay Lerner and Frederick Loewe composed the musical *My Fair Lady*. During lively luncheons in the 1920s, legendary editor Harold Ross conceived of *New Yorker* magazine, and one of his tablemates, Dorothy Parker, is thought to still visit the Algonquin.

In 1919, a group of theater critics, columnists, and actors began a tradition of lunching over shared opinions, ideas, and witticisms. Alexander Woollcott, seen at left in a Carl Van Vechten photograph, and Dorothy Parker (below) joined Harold Ross, Robert Benchley, and Robert E. Sherwood at the Algonquin Hotel daily. They called themselves the Vicious Circle but are remembered as the Round Table. Parker, a poet, wrote book reviews for the *New Yorker* and coauthored *A Star is Born*. After two unsuccessful suicide attempts, Parker died of natural causes in 1967 at the age of 73, and that is when paranormal activity began to be reported at the hotel. Staff and guests have reported hearing furniture being moved and objects being relocated. People have seen shadows out of the corner of their eyes and even a full-body apparition of Parker walking across the lobby and then vanishing.

Hotel Thirty Thirty, the towering Renaissance Revival building seen at right, began as the Martha Washington Hotel, which was for women only. When 34-year-old English woman Eileen Courtis rented a room on the 12th floor, she realized she was not alone. Night after night, she would awaken to the sound of rustling papers, followed by footsteps across the floor; but when she turned on the lights, all was quiet. One night, she panicked when she woke and felt unable to move her arms or legs. Only after she moved to another floor did she learn that two former residents had died in her old room.

Ghostly tales abound about the Chelsea Hotel at 222 West Twenty-third Street. Built in 1884, the Chelsea operates as both a residence and a hotel. Mark Twain and O. Henry (William Sydney Porter) were the first of many writers to find their muse there. Eugene O'Neill, Tennessee Williams, and Dylan Thomas followed. In the 1960s, musicians like Janis Joplin and Bob Dylan visited. After Thomas's death in 1953, his specter appeared to a resident in room 206. Nancy Spungen, the girlfriend and manager of rocker Sid Vicious of the Sex Pistols, died in her Chelsea bathroom after sustaining multiple stab wounds. Vicious was arraigned for the murder but died of a drug overdose before the trial. His ghost has been reported around the first-floor elevator. Loud music and the sound of a couple arguing have been heard coming from the murder room. Residents and staff still hear occasional screams or footsteps down empty corridors, only to discover furniture rearranged and lights turned on or off; but they are not surprised, knowing the passionate energy that has passed through the stately Victorian building.

The Ansonia Hotel attracted famous tenants after it opened in 1904. Enrico Caruso, Arturo Toscanini, Florenz Ziegfeld Jr., Igor Stravinsky, and Babe Ruth enjoyed the grand ballroom, tearooms, and what was the world's largest indoor pool while living in the Beaux Arts–style residence. The lobby featured a fountain with live seals, and on warm summer nights, an orchestra performed on the roof. On Christmas Eve 2003, Maurice D. Valentine, an employee of The North Face outdoor store, located inside the landmark hotel, was tidying up the men's department when a man appeared. The man's handlebar mustache, big-brimmed hat, and long, dark cloak looked old-fashioned. He walked with purpose and then vanished. The once-skeptical Valentine stood in dumb wonder. Later, fortified with drink, he shared his experience with a coworker and learned that other employees had experienced inexplicable things as well. Others saw the mysterious man, heard party noises after closing, and found objects that had moved. Apparently, the hauntings are not limited to the store, as Ansonia residents have also seen various apparitions over the years.

Both ghosts and murder have visited the Dakota apartments. After Edward Clark (left) rolled out his plan for an elegant apartment building at West Seventy-second Street, critics called it "Clark's folly." When someone likened the remote location to the Dakota Territories, Clark adopted the name. The wood-paneled rooms and high ceilings attracted film legends Lauren Bacall, Judy Garland, and Boris Karloff. Its gabled roof and ornamental details of griffins set the stage for the haunted activity inside. One specter that has been seen is Clark, who continues to oversee his beloved building and has appeared to workmen and an electrician in years past. Some people think that seeing the ghost of a little girl in a yellow taffeta dress, as some have, portends death. Ghosts of a crying lady and a little boy have also been seen.

When John Lennon and his wife, Yoko Ono, moved into the Dakota apartment once belonging to actor Robert Ryan (right), they experienced strange phenomena and reportedly conducted a séance. With a medium's help, they connected with Ryan's deceased wife, Jessie, who had died of cancer there, and she expressed her intention of remaining in her home. Lennon also died at the Dakota, on December 8, 1980, when Mark David Chapman murdered him at the Dakota entrance. Lennon and Ono alighted from their limousine, and as they approached the gate, Chapman rushed in and fired five shots, four of which struck Lennon in the shoulder and back. The hospital declared him dead on arrival at 11:07 p.m. Afterward, Ono and others claimed they saw Lennon's apparition.

The land that Gracie Mansion sits on has evolved over the years. George Washington used the first country house on this site as a fort during the Revolutionary War, until the British captured it and burned it down. Archibald Gracie built the present Federal-style summerhouse in 1799. When the parks department acquired the house in 1896 and turned it into an ice cream stand (above), it had a haunted reputation, with sightings of a specter named Elizabeth Stoughton Wolcolt, Gracie's daughter-in-law, who had suffered a stroke and died there on June 26, 1819. The house then became the first home of the Museum of the City of New York from 1924 to 1930. After the mansion underwent a renovation (below), parks commissioner Robert Moses persuaded the city to designate it the official residence of the mayor in 1942.

History remembers Elizabeth Bowen Jumel (right) as an adventuress, prostitute, madam, and murderer. In 1804, using her beauty and a bit of deception, she married wine merchant Stephen Jumel and became the wealthiest woman in North America. In 1810, the Jumels bought the Robert Morris mansion (below) on 160th Street. Despite their grand home and lavish furnishings, New York society rejected Elizabeth. Some speculate that Aaron Burr caught her eye because of his former position of vice president, and they began an affair. In 1832, Jumel's husband suffered injuries in a carriage accident and died. The following year, she married Burr. Stephen Jumel's spirit, speaking through mediums, has claimed that his wife ripped his bandages off his wounds, letting him bleed out, and, with a doctor's help, had him buried alive.

MADAME JUMEL

43

Lt. Col. Robert Morris built what became the Jumels' house, the oldest home still standing in Manhattan, in 1765. A British loyalist, Morris abandoned the house during the Revolutionary War. George Washington, and later the British army, used the mansion as a headquarters. In 1993, visitors reported seeing the specter of a Revolutionary soldier on the top floor.

The house earned its haunted reputation as early as 1868, just three years after Elizabeth Jumel's death at the age of 70. A governess staying at the house reported residents being woken nightly between 12:00 a.m. and 1:00 a.m. to the sound of loud rapping noises. One night, she awoke to disturbing noises in the Lafayette Room, seen here. Tapping noises moved around the walls to the windowpanes.

Many apparitions have been seen at the Jumel house over the last 100 years. In the early days, Stephen Jumel's phantom lurked in the hallways. His apparition has not been seen since he told of his murder during one séance. The ghost of a servant girl has been seen on the top floor, near where she threw herself to her death from a window. Even Aaron Burr has appeared to some, despite having lived in the home only four months. However, Elizabeth Jumel's apparition appears the most. In one incident, she startled a group of visiting students when she appeared on the balcony above the door wearing an old-fashioned purple gown.

Gay Street, in Greenwich Village, features some of the oldest homes in Manhattan, with houses on the west (left) side of the street dating to 1833 and houses on the east (right) side dating to 1844. In the 1800s, freed slaves lived on the short street. While residing in the basement apartment of 14 Gay Street, Ruth McKenney penned a series of stories published in the *New Yorker* that were later adapted into a play, a film, and the Broadway musical *Wonderful Town*. All the reported haunted activity is centered 12 Gay Street. Over the years, residents have claimed to hear party sounds coming from the house late at night. The laughter and strains of lively music are attributed to the 1920s, when the Pirates Den, a speakeasy, occupied the basement during Prohibition. One owner, Walter Gibson, saw two apparitions in the 1940s, one well-dressed man who walked down the front steps and vanished at the street and another dressed in evening attire in the house.

Another owner at 12 Gay Street, puppeteer Frank Paris, stated that pounding noises and heavy footsteps on the stairs had woken him many times. He too saw the apparitions and reportedly held a séance, connecting with the spirit of a man who died when a horse-drawn carriage ran him down on the way to his daughter's wedding.

People say disgraced mayor Jimmy Walker has joined the other spirits at 12 Gay Street. Walker bought the house to be close to his mistress, Betty Compton, whom he later married. They are seen here together in 1836. The city prospered when Walker became mayor in 1926. However, his reputation for chorus girls and accepting bribes caught up to him during his second term, and he resigned from office in 1932.

Bank Street, in Greenwich Village, earned its name after yellow fever epidemics drove Wall Street businesses to temporarily relocate to the safer air uptown. The quiet street lined with historic homes seems an incongruous place for the city's financial hub, let alone ghosts and murderers. Between West Fourth and Bleecker Streets lived the suspected Boston Strangler, Charles E. Terry (see page 78). Across the street from Terry, rocker and accused murderer Sid Vicious died from a drug overdose. Closer to Greenwich Avenue lived Dr. Harvey Slatin, an engineer, and his wife in the 1950s, who, after beginning renovations, heard tapping and footsteps on the floors above when no one was there. After their carpenter found a tin box containing the cremated remains of Elizabeth Bullock, who died in 1931, the activity increased. Slatin enlisted the aid of famous ghost investigator Hans Holzer. During a séance, Bullock, a Catholic, communicated that her family had disowned her after she married a Protestant, so, upon her death, her husband stole and hid her ashes. Telling her story seemed to release the spirit because the activity stopped.

In 1997, Ye Waverly Inn became another paranormal hot spot on Bank Street. In December of that year, the *New York Times* featured a story about the unusual activity at the charming restaurant. The building began in 1844 as a carriage house and then became a bordello and a popular tavern. The poet Robert Frost, seen here, regularly enjoyed the inn's warm fireplace. The restaurant's cuisine still attracts celebrities today. In the *Times* story, some employees admitted to experiencing strange occurrences such as lights turning on and off, unknown footsteps on the stairs after closing, and the apparition of a man in formal clothes. However, the principle focus of the article was a mysterious fire that occurred in December, just before Christmas. The fire marshal said investigators had determined the exact location that the fire began, but they could not figure out what sparked the blaze, as there were no signs of accelerants, no combustibles, and no electrical outlets in the area. Another fire of indeterminate cause occurred on June 25, 2012. Both fires did little damage to the restaurant and only added to its mystique.

The picturesque charm of Greenwich Village's Tenth Street belies its haunted history. Built in 1857, Tenth Street Studios (above), located at 51 West Tenth Street, established Greenwich Village as a gathering place for artists in New York City. The building housed the first architecture school in the United States, run by the building's designer, Richard Morris Hunt. Prominent artists, including Winslow Homer and Frederic Church, worked and held exhibitions there. In the 1940s, a group of modernist painters and sculptors called the Bombshell Artists met in the cellar. Another tenant, John LaFarge (left), a painter, muralist, and master with stained glass, startled people by reportedly walking through walls there after his death in 1910. He has also been seen admiring the mural he painted at the Church of the Ascension, at the corner of Tenth Street and Fifth Avenue.

Author and actress Jan Bryant Bartell wrote the book *Spindrift: Spray From a Psychic Sea*, detailing her many strange experiences while living on the beloved Tenth Street. Plagued by oppressive shadows, footsteps, the sound of breaking china, and repeated visits by the ghost she came to call "the lady in white," Bartell left the neighborhood, only to return three and a half years later, moving into the house next door to where the frightening activity had occurred. Peace eluded her there as well when she became convinced the house was cursed after death had visited nine of the 10 families living there. Shortly after leaving, Bartell became the 10th. About 20 years later, five-year-old Lisa Steinberg died after suffering physical abuse at the hands of Joel Steinberg while living in the house. Her death echoed claims of a similar child murder that happened there in the 1930s.

COPYRIGHTED BY
A.F.BRADLEY.
NEW YORK . 1907.

Tour guides call the Bartells' former apartment building the House of Death. Built in 1855, its most famous resident was Samuel Clemens, better known as Mark Twain, who occupied it in 1900, when it was still a single-family home. A nonbeliever in the paranormal, he did admit that, on one occasion, upon entering the fireplace storage room, he saw wood moving on its own accord. Clemens moved out after only one year, explaining that his wife could not keep up with the housekeeping. Others said that his wife had a nervous breakdown because of an oppressive energy in the building. The house was converted to apartments in 1938, and a resident on the ground floor moved out after she encountered a white-haired man in her living room who said his name was Clemens and that he a had problem there he had to fix.

Three

THE FAMOUS AND
THE INFAMOUS

Prior to his winning the Noble Prize for Peace, prior to the building of the Panama Canal, and prior to his ascension to the US presidency, Theodore "Teddy" Roosevelt Jr. served two years as the president of the board of New York City Police Commissioners, starting in 1895. Although his reign was short, he was effective. He assumed his role following a probe conducted by the state senate revealed widespread corruption.

During Roosevelt's tenure as president of the board of police commissioners, he established disciplinary rules and merit awards. He started the practice of appointing recruits based on mental and physical prowess, rather than political connections. Roosevelt rode his bike or walked different beats in the city to ensure that policemen did not shirk their duties or sneak into bars to drink. After Roosevelt died in 1919, he reportedly continued to check up on the men at their new headquarters at 240 Centre Street. The department occupied the Beaux Arts–style building (above) from 1909 until 1973, and many policemen admitted to similar strange experiences while working there. An officer working at his desk would feel he was being watched. Upon looking up, he would see a short, intense man staring at him, who then disappeared. The man, they all agreed, looked like Teddy Roosevelt.

In 1888, Thomas F. Byrnes, the head of the department of New York police detectives, appeared a bit arrogant when he criticized London's handling of the Jack the Ripper murders, saying that if the same happened in New York, the killer would be caught. On January 19, 1889, the East Thirty-fifth Street police station received a letter signed "Jack the Ripper," stating that he had come to America. When the body of Carrie Brown was discovered on the morning of April 24, 1891, the *New York Times* headline screamed "Choked, Then Mutilated; A Murder Like One of 'Jack the Ripper's' Deeds." Under intense pressure, Byrnes arrested a dark-skinned, black-haired Algerian man nicknamed Frenchy, despite a witness's description that the man with Carrie Brown had a light-colored mustache. Convicted, Frenchy was pardoned 11 years later, owing to police misconduct. Brown's murder remains unsolved. Interestingly, the rest of the murderer's description—a sharp nose and slim build, wearing a brown cutaway coat and black trousers—resembles witness descriptions of London's Jack the Ripper.

One of the first sensationalized murders in Manhattan caught Edgar Allen Poe's attention. He became so interested in the case that the police even considered him a suspect for a time. On July 25, 1841, Mary Rogers left her home at 126 Nassau Street, seen here in the early 1900s, and never returned. Three days later, she was found floating in the Hudson River. According to police, her body indicated that a violent attack had occurred. Many reporters knew Rogers, who worked at a cigar shop near Newspaper Row, and referred to her as the "beautiful cigar girl."

Newspapers covered the Mary Rogers case extensively because she was friends with so many reporters. On October 7, 1841, less than three months after her death, the body of her fiancé, Daniel Payne, was found along the river's edge with a bottle of poison by his side and a note that did not mention Rogers's murder but ended with, "God forgive me for my misspent life." Later, a story surfaced that a tavern keeper on her deathbed said that Rogers had visited her establishment and met a doctor who performed an abortion on Rogers that resulted in her death. The tavern keeper's son helped to dispose of the body in the Hudson River. The police refuted that story, saying that the medical examiner had determined that Rogers was a virgin when she died and that her throat bore the signs of strangulation. The case remains unsolved, but Poe, in 1842, published his theory of the murder in the form of a short story entitled "The Mystery of Marie Rogêt." The illustration from that story is seen here.

War hero, lawyer, attorney general, and vice president Aaron Burr accomplished much in his 80 years of life. He is seen at left at age 77. In death, he has reportedly been active at many locations. Since 1836, people have seen his apparition at his former residences, 3 Wall Street and the Morris-Jumel mansion, and at his stable, once located at 110 West Third Street. Burr's former carriage house, now the upscale restaurant One If By Land, Two if by Sea at 17 Barrow Street, has experienced chairs, napkins, and tools moving about and people being touched. The building's cellar once housed Burr's dead daughter's belongings. He grieved hard when Theodosia Burr Alston's ship disappeared in December 1812 while en route to New York. His apparition has also been seen in Battery Park (seen here in the 1890s), staring out into the harbor, awaiting his daughter's return.

On December 4, 1891, at the Arcade building (above, second on the left), a redheaded man presented a letter to the offices of successful broker Russell Sage (right). Seeing that the note demanded $1 million, Sage flatly refused. The redheaded man then pulled a shiny pistol from his coat and throwing his satchel to the ground, fired into it. Sage grabbed a visitor, William Laidlaw, and thrust him between the intruder and himself. A flash and rumble preceded the explosion, which catapulted one clerk out of a window to his death. Only the head remained of the redheaded man, who was later identified as Henry Norcross. The crippled Laidlaw sued Sage for using him as a human shield. After multiple favorable judgments and appeals, Laidlaw finally lost on a technicality. Sage died in 1906, leaving an estate worth more than $8 million.

59

Mathew Brady (left) became known in the mid-1800s for capturing the faces of famous people with his camera lens. His photographs of Abraham Lincoln were the models for the $5 bill and the Lincoln penny. In all, 18 US presidents sat for him. He began by studying portrait painting and then met Louis Jacques Daguerre, the inventor of daguerreotype photography. After studying avidly and winning awards for his work, Brady opened his first studio (below) at 55 Broadway in 1844, followed by a second one in Washington, DC, in 1849. An advertisement he placed in the *New York Herald* was the first to use a different font from that of the publication, making his notice stand out and setting a trend for future newspaper advertisements.

History remembers Mathew Brady most for being a pioneer of photojournalism during the Civil War. His images, like the one above, brought the gory realities of war and death to the public. As a result, the US government outlawed war photography during World War I and limited what could be shown in future wars. Unfortunately, his Civil War passion bankrupted Brady, as the government chose not to purchase any of his photographs; ironically, many are now part of the National Archives. Brady died poor in 1896, but he did have the distinction of being buried in the Congressional Cemetery in Washington, DC. For the next 100 years, people have reportedly seen Brady with his walking stick gliding from his New York studio up Broadway to St. Paul's Church. Other accounts describe bright flashes, like those from a camera, spotted in the area of his studio.

John Wilkes Booth (left) shot a bullet into the back of the head of Pres. Abraham Lincoln (below) on April 14, 1865, at Ford's Theater in Washington, DC. Booth had achieved financial success as an actor, following his family's theatrical trade, but, unlike his famous older brother Edwin, who was a Unionist, John Wilkes supported the Confederacy. He felt the assassination would provide the Confederacy the chance to continue the war. When Lincoln died the next day at 7:22 a.m., the nation plunged into mourning. A profoundly silent funeral procession was followed with a public viewing at the Capitol rotunda. On April 21, Lincoln's body began a journey by train to its final resting place in Springfield, Illinois.

After arriving in New York City by ferry, President Lincoln's casket was transported to city hall. An estimated 120,000 citizens waited in line for hours to view the body. The next day, on April 25, a procession of 60,000 to 100,00 people accompanied the wagon that conveyed the body, drawn by 16 horses, up Broadway to the Hudson River Railway depot at Thirtieth Street. At journey's end, Lincoln's body traveled by train through seven states on a route similar to the one he had taken following his first election. Stories spread in the years after the funeral of people seeing the appearance of the ghost train on or near the anniversary dates of the 1865 trip. Uniformed skeletons were reportedly seen guarding the coffin. People in New York City claim to have seen the steam engine coming from the south on the former tracks of the New York Central Railroad.

A syndicate of wealthy men built the second Madison Square Garden (seen here) in 1890 on Twenty-sixth Street, overlooking Madison Square Park. The architect, Stanford White, incorporated Moorish characteristics in the Beaux Arts structure. White occupied a studio in the tower for his work, and he was killed at the rooftop restaurant on June 25, 1906.

Stanford White, born in New York in 1853, studied architecture in Europe. Using elements of the Italian Renaissance style, he created a new style called Free Classical. In addition to Madison Square Garden, he designed banks, the Boston Public Library, the Washington Square Arch, and private residences, making him rich in the 1890s. Although he was married, at age 47, he grew interested in 16-year-old model and showgirl Evelyn Nesbit. He convinced Nesbit's mother he wanted only to be a benefactor.

STANFORD WHITE

64

Evelyn Nesbit's beauty and talent attracted Stanford White. An artist first discovered her at the age of 14 and turned her into the most recognizable fashion model of the period. Growing up poor and fatherless, she must have been dazzled by White's wealth. When her mother went out of town, White plied her with alcohol and took her virginity.

Nesbit also gained the attention of millionaire Harry K. Thaw, who had a history of mental illness. When Nesbit appeared in a show called *The Wild Rose*, Thaw attended 40 performances and begged to marry her. Knowing that he valued chastity, she divulged her experiences with White. The revelation unhinged him, and he then imprisoned, beat, and raped her. Despite her ordeal, Nesbit still married Thaw, knowing that her reputation had been ruined because of White.

On June 25, 1906, Harry K. Thaw booked tickets to a revue at Madison Square Garden's rooftop restaurant. At the last minute, Stanford White changed his plans and took his regular seat to watch the show. At 11:00 p.m., Thaw approached White from behind and fired three times, killing him instantly. Raising the gun high in triumph, Thaw allowed himself to be carried to the Tombs prison, where crowds gathered. Newspapers dubbed his case the "Trial of the Century," and it ended in a hung jury. Jurors are seen below. His second jury found him guilty by reason of insanity. He never regretted the killing, convincing himself he had avenged his wife's honor.

Although he had been sentenced to life at the Matteawan State Hospital for the criminally insane, Harry Thaw was declared sane on July 16, 1915. The following December, Thaw met 18-year-old Frederick Gump in Kansas City. He then earned the trust of Gump's family, convincing them he would pay for their son's education. Gump arrived in New York City on Christmas Eve 1916, and Thaw directed him to the Hotel McAlpin, seen here.

Early on Christmas morning, Thaw entered Gump's bedroom and attacked the boy, whipping him into a bloody mess. Thaw then stepped out, leaving his bodyguard in charge, but Gump escaped. Thaw went into hiding at this boardinghouse in Philadelphia. On January 11, 1917, he attempted suicide by slashing his throat, after which he was sent to Kirkbride Asylum in Philadelphia until 1924. He died in 1947 at age 76.

When Clyde Fitch's last play, *The City*, opened at the Lyric Theatre (later reconstructed as Foxwoods Theatre) on December 21, 1909, audience members fainted. Some stated it was because the word "goddamn" was spoken for the first time in a Broadway play. Other reports recounted that Fitch appeared onstage during the final curtain call, took a bow, and then vanished. Fitch had died more than three months before, on September 4. His face would have been recognizable to the audience, as he had earned much fame as a playwright. He died at age 44 after writing more than 62 plays. The first playwright to publish his own work, he once had five shows running concurrently on Broadway. Although the public flocked to his shows, he did not earn critical acclaim until *The City*, which could explain why he came back for that final bow.

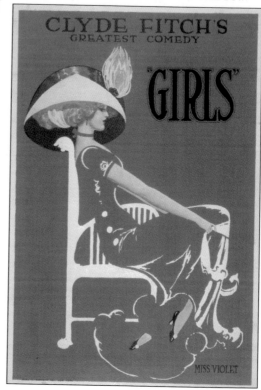

At 2:00 a.m. on July 16, 1912, while the streets in the Tenderloin district teemed with prostitutes and gamblers, an expectant hush fell over Forty-third Street between Sixth Avenue and Broadway. Halfway down the block, the rhythmic idle of a Packard covered the sound of footsteps as dark-suited men crept into the shadows of the Hotel Metropole. When the pudgy Herman Rosenthal stepped out of the hotel, he ate a bullet. A second slug cut a path through his brain.

A crowd gathered to watch Rosenthal's coffin loaded into the hearse, but most were glad to see him dead. After pimping his wife and promoting fights, Rosenthal had ventured into gambling. He garnered the assistance of Tammany politician "Big Tim" Sullivan, an enigma of a man who funded criminal organizations while supporting women's rights and gun control. However, Rosenthal learned too late that, in order to succeed, he needed to pad the pockets of the police.

After authorities raided his gambling joint at 104 West Forty-fifth Street, Rosenthal took the unprecedented step of partnering with a policeman, Lt. Charles Becker (left), who was in charge of vice. Becker's planned 20-percent cut ended when police commissioner Rhinelander Waldo (below) insisted that Becker raid Rosenthal again. The police lieutenant promised to reimburse the gambler but instead followed his superior's order and posted an officer on the gambler's doorstep. Rosenthal's angry response started the machinations that led to his execution. He gave two sworn affidavits to the popular *New York World* newspaper, detailing his partnership with Charles Becker and accusing other officers of graft. The city's district attorney, Charles Whitman, took notice and agreed to hear Rosenthal's complaints, but he informed the gambler that he needed corroborating witnesses. Rosenthal promised to return at 7:00 a.m. the next morning, but a gun ended his plans.

Police found the Packard, its driver, and the man who hired him, "Bald Jack" Rose (seen here), Charles Becker's right-hand man. Rose had grown wealthy by collecting protection fees from illegal businesses for Becker. This connection, coupled with Rosenthal's allegations, spelled the end of Charles Becker. District attorney Charles Whitman exchanged immunity for Rose's testimony against Becker.

Rose admitted to hiring and paying members of the Jewish Lenox Gang to carry out the hit on Rosenthal. When Whitney Lewis, Dago Frank Cirofisi, Harry "Gyp the Blood" Horowitz (seated, left), and "Lefty" Louis Rosenberg (seated, right) stood trial, they professed their innocence. It took less than 30 minutes to convict the four of first-degree murder and the same amount of time to execute them on April 13, 1914.

Charles Becker's first trial resulted in a first-degree murder conviction and a death sentence. Seen at left in 1914, Becker has reason to smile, as the court of appeals overturned his conviction, citing that the judge had been prejudiced against the defendant. District attorney Charles Whitman won a retrial, and despite Jack Rose's personal motive for wanting Rosenthal dead and admitting to setting up the hit, he again testified for the prosecution. The press convicted Becker, and the second jury followed suit. On July 30, 1915, Becker went to Sing Sing prison's electric chair (seen below in 1915), professing his innocence, and many believed him. Stoic to the end, Becker suffered a cruel death, as the voltage heated his body to 140 degrees but did not kill him. With flames at his temples, he suffered three jolts over nine minutes before dying.

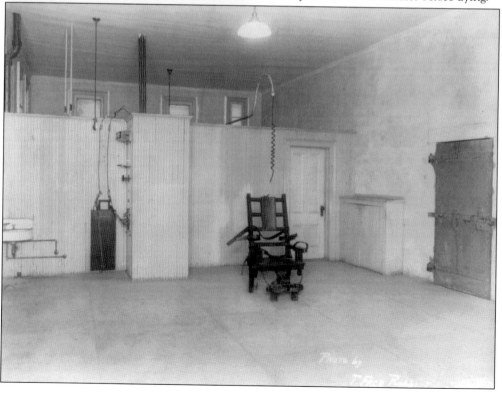

Arnold Rothstein (above) achieved success in the underworld by using his brain over brawn. Some historians credit him for establishing organized crime. Gamblers like Herman Rosenthal looked to him for loans, and gangsters relied on him to mediate disputes. The reported mastermind of the 1919 "Black Sox" World Series scandal, Rothstein owned interests in speakeasies and gambling houses. When he was gunned down in front of the Park Central Hotel on November 4, 1928, some said he had failed to pay a gambling debt. Others claimed that Dutch Schultz funded the hit because he blamed Rothstein for the murder of Schultz's partner, Joey Noe, in October 1928.

Vincent "Mad Dog" Coll (above, center) smiles for the press after being acquitted of murder in 1931. Coll's criminal activities began early when he joined a Hell's Kitchen gang called the Gophers. Later, he became the hit man for Dutch Schultz. When Coll demanded to be a partner, Schultz denied him, sparking a feud. Coll earned income by kidnapping other gangsters for ransom. This earned him countless enemies and bounties on his head. He finally met his end at the London Chemist drugstore, in a phone booth. Owney "The Killer" Madden, the head of the Irish Hell's Kitchen mob, apparently orchestrated the hit. Madden kept Coll on the phone long enough for the call to be traced. A man armed with a submachine gun then arrived and filled him with 15 bullets. No one stood trial for Coll's murder, but Dutch Schultz sent condolence flowers.

Dutch Schultz began as a burglar, but he made his fortune as a bootlegger. Seen here before his death in 1935, he used brutality to gain control over rival territories. When Schultz and his partner, Joey Noe, moved into Manhattan, a gang war broke out with Jack "Legs" Diamond. When Noe died in 1928 after being shot on Fifty-fourth Street, Schultz allegedly enlisted George "Hump" McManus to kill Diamond's close associate, Arnold Rothstein, in retaliation. Schultz lived on to beat a tax evasion indictment brought by US attorney Thomas Dewey. Seeking revenge again, Schultz went before the Mafia commission requesting permission to kill Dewey. The board refused and subsequently had Schultz gunned down on October 23, 1935, at the Palace Chophouse in Newark. While waiting for an ambulance to take him to the hospital, he drank brandy to mitigate the pain. He lasted 22 hours before expiring.

The gunmen who murdered Malcolm X (left) at Harlem's Audubon Ballroom killed a messenger for the unification of the races. This new vision of unification came at the end of his life. As a child, he witnessed racism and violence against his family. He believed various white supremacist groups were responsible for the loss of his home, his father, and three uncles. He grew interested in the teachings of the Nation of Islam in 1948 while serving time in jail. With his passion and charisma, he grew into a leadership role for the group and was credited for increasing membership from 500 to 30,0000 over 11 years. He eventually split from the Nation because of certain actions by the organization's leader, Elijah Muhammad. After a trip around the world, Malcolm X's ideas evolved, and he began pushing for racial integration. The assassins at the Audubon Ballroom silenced him. The stage is seen below after the murder.

On Valentine's Day, 1965, Malcolm X and his family survived a firebombing of their home. Seven days later, on February 21, as he took the stage of the Audubon Ballroom, three gunmen rushed the stage and shot him 15 times. The doctors at Columbia Presbyterian Hospital declared Malcolm X dead at 3:30 p.m. The audience grabbed one of the gunmen, Talmadge Hayer, and beat him until authorities arrived. Police captured the other two murderers, Norman 3X Butler and Thomas 15X Johnson. The three members of the Nation of Islam were convicted of first-degree murder and have since been paroled. Somewhere between 14,000 and 30,000 people attended a public viewing at the Unity Funeral Home (above) in Harlem from February 23 to February 26, 1965.

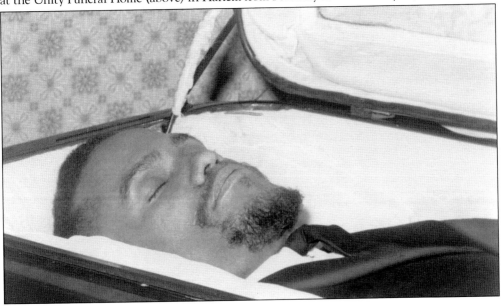

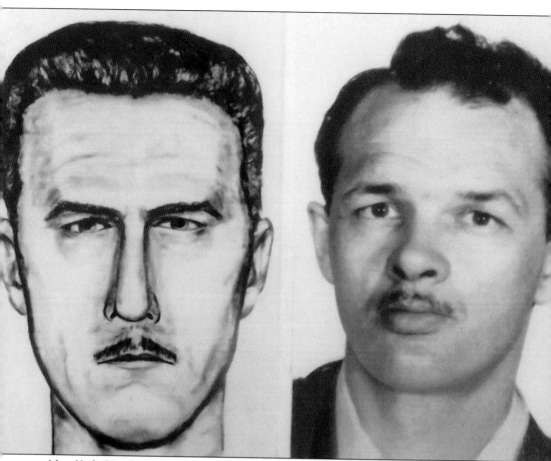

New York City detective Thomas Cavanagh Jr. solved the first six Boston strangling murders but died before he could be proven right. After finding Zenovia Clegg strangled to death in May 1963 at the Woodstock Hotel in Times Square, Cavanagh used this sketch to track down Charles E. Terry. Cavanagh learned that Terry had lived in Boston from 1961 until August 30, 1962, which coincided with the first six Boston murders, and he noticed similarities between those killings and Clegg's. The victims were all strangled with a ligature tied into an elaborate bow. They were all over the age of 50, their bodies were all staged and violated in a macabre fashion, and all the crime scenes were ransacked but nothing was taken. Terry confessed to Clegg's murder but refused to talk with Boston detectives. Albert DeSalvo, jailed for other crimes, later confessed but never stood trial for the Boston murders. On November 24, 1973, DeSalvo said he wanted to tell the truth, but he was murdered that night. After Cavanagh retired, he attempted to reopen the cases, but he died on August 2, 1996, without proving his assertion.

Four

CHURCHES, MUSEUMS, AND MYSTERIOUS INSTITUTIONS

St. Patrick's Old Cathedral, dedicated on May 14, 1815, was the seat of the Archdiocese of New York until the new St. Patrick's Cathedral opened on May 25, 1879. Located at 263 Mulberry Street, the old cathedral supported much of the immigrant population that first settled on the Lower East Side. Worshippers are seen here leaving Sunday services in January 1943. Visitors claim that ghosts cling to the old house of worship.

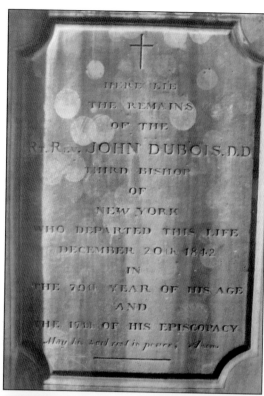

One of the specters wandering St. Patrick's Old Cathedral is thought to be the third bishop of New York City, John DuBois. When he died, he asked to be buried beneath the entrance on the Mott Street side of the church. His apparition has reportedly been seen both in the church and outside in the graveyard. Another recognizable ghost is Pierre Toussaint, a Haitian slave and church member, whose charitable deeds earned him the consideration of sainthood. Although his family remains in the graveyard, Toussaint's body was moved to the new St. Patrick's Cathedral crypt. Toussaint and DuBois are not alone. Other spirits have reportedly appeared as mist-like forms, hovering around the graves, still drawing comfort from the spiritual surroundings.

The graveyards of Manhattan reveal the island's history. The weathered tombstones in Trinity Wall Street's churchyard escaped the modernization of the city towering over it, while fire and poor construction destroyed two former churches there. The existing church, built in 1846 in the Gothic Revival style, with a 280-foot spire, was the tallest landmark in Manhattan for 44 years. It also reportedly became home to notable ghosts, who walked its graveyard.

Founding father Alexander Hamilton (left) died after being shot in a duel with Vice Pres. Aaron Burr. They were both war heroes, lawyers, and had each established banks and newspapers, yet Burr felt Hamilton impeded his attempts at political advancement. Their conflict turned deadly when Hamilton made public comments suggesting that Burr was having an incestuous relationship with his daughter Theodosia. After Hamilton refused to apologize, Burr challenged him to a duel.

The Aaron Burr-Alexander Hamilton duel commenced on the muggy morning of July 11, 1804. Hamilton opposed dueling, as his oldest son had died in a duel, yet he chose to answer Burr's claims of slander. Historians disagree as to who fired first, but one account described Burr's bullet striking Hamilton in the abdomen. The impact then reportedly spun him, and Hamilton's firearm harmlessly discharged as he fell to the ground.

Burr hid his face with a handkerchief when attendants collected Hamilton's unconscious body. Before dying, Hamilton grabbed someone at his bedside and supposedly said, "Tell them I did not intend to fire." He died at 2:15 p.m. on July 12, 1804, yet people have reported seeing him in the graveyard of Trinity Wall Street, standing and staring at his monument with an expression described as morose.

Hamilton is not the only ghost that walks Trinity's graveyard. Robert Fulton, in his youth, traveled to Europe, where he became fascinated with mechanical ships and earned a commission from Napoleon Bonaparte to build the first practical submarine, called the *Nautilus*. Fulton earned fame after launching the *North River Steamboat*, later referred to as the *Clermont*, on the Hudson River in New York City on August 17, 1807.

When the *North River Steamboat* started its journey against the current to Albany, New York City fishermen, unfamiliar with steam engines, cowered in terror, thinking they were seeing a monster. Fulton continues to startle people today, as many have reported seeing his specter in Trinity's graveyard. His visitations seem to occur only when the harbor is closed to traffic. Sightings were reported often during the world wars and in the weeks following the World Trade Center terrorist attacks on September 11, 2001.

A neighborhood, a housing project, and a high school bear the name of Peter Stuyvesant, the Dutch director-general. He ruled the colony of New Netherland, including the settlement of New Amsterdam, from 1647 until surrendering it to the British in 1664, when it was renamed New York. He lived out his final years on the 300-acre farm he had purchased in 1651. It encompassed what is now the East Village, from the East River to Fourth Avenue and from Fifth Street to Seventeenth Street. When he died, he was buried in the family chapel on the property. The Stuyvesant descendants, upon donating the land to the local parish, stipulated that the church must care for the family vault. Reportedly, St. Mark's Church in the Bowery also inherited the ghost of Peter Stuyvesant. People have recognized him for his distinctive Dutch attire and his limping stride due to his wooden leg.

Since the building of St. Mark's Church in the Bowery in 1799, the ghost of Peter Stuyvesant has reportedly made regular visits. Change seems to provoke his hauntings. In the 1830s, when houses and roads were under construction on his former land near the church, workers reported hearing tapping and moaning. On another evening, neighbors heard the church bell ringing inside the empty building. The bell supposedly rang again, unaided, on the night of Abraham Lincoln's assassination. Many people continue to claim to see his specter or hear the tap-shuffle of his peg leg in the church or graveyard. However, his is not the only ghost of St. Mark's. The apparition of a woman has appeared in the balcony near the organ, near the rear entrance, and in the center section of the nave during church services.

St. Paul's Chapel (left) survived the fire of 1776 and the destruction of the World Trade Center on September 11, 2001. George Washington attended services there after his presidential inauguration. Constructed in 1766, St. Paul's is the oldest public building in continuous use in the city, and it has a haunted graveyard. George Frederick Cooke is buried in one of the 17th-century graves. An English actor, Cooke gained fame and rave reviews after performing the role of Richard III at the Park Lane Theater (below). In private life, Cooke gambled and drank, and when he ran out of money, he sold his head for research. Since his death, a headless apparition has been seen wandering St. Paul's graveyard and down in nearby Theater Alley, the former site of the Park Lane Theater. Many suppose he is looking for his head, or his former glory.

Sometimes, inexplicable events come out of ordinary lives. The *New York Times* dubbed the Merchant's House Museum "Manhattan's Most Haunted House," yet no murders or suicides mar its history. Seabury Tredwell moved into the three-year-old house in 1835, and his family occupied it until his daughter, Gertrude, died in 1933. A distant relative, George Chapman, turned the property into a museum in 1936. (Courtesy of Merchant's House Museum.)

More than 3,000 items of clothing, furniture, and personal possessions belonging to the Tredwells are still in the Greek Revival rooms, giving visitors an authentic experience of life in the mid-1800s. In 1934, the year following Gertrude's death, the apparition of a stern, elderly woman startled a museum consultant as she evaluated clothing belonging to the family. (Courtesy of Merchant's House Museum.)

Sightings of a female apparition have occurred many times since the opening of the Merchant's House Museum. Witnesses described the woman they saw as either elderly or young but always dressed in period clothing. At first referred to as the Lady in White, the woman often appeared near the front door. Many believed it to be Gertrude Tredwell, the youngest child of Seabury Tredwell. After one failed love affair, she never married and spent her entire life in the house. In her lifetime, women often learned to play the piano, so when reports arose of ghostly music coming from the pianoforte in the parlor, many assumed Gertrude was making her presence known. (Courtesy of Merchant's House Museum.)

Gertrude is not the only Tredwell who has been seen in the house. In the mid-1980s, an apparition of the patriarch of the family, Seabury, frightened three men. Minutes after beginning their self-guided tour, they hurried down from the second floor and reported that an older gentleman blocked their way. The story puzzled staff members, as no other visitors were in the house. On their way out, one guest pointed to Seabury's portrait hanging in the parlor, saying that was the man they had seen. The painting figured in another incident in 2002, when a school group toured the house. One boy exploring ahead of his group came back and refused to go into the front bedroom because he said the man in the picture downstairs was standing by the bed. Gertrude and Seabury Tredwell both died in the front bedroom. (Courtesy of Merchant's House Museum.)

As was the custom in the Victorian era, married couples occupied separate bedrooms. These rooms in the Merchant's House Museum continue to be active. In Eliza's bedroom, the bed sometimes appears to be slept in. People often capture unusual light anomalies and defects in their photographs taken there, and during investigations conducted by Sturges Paranormal, electronic voice phenomena (EVPs) have been recorded. In this same bedroom, an unsettling event happened on October 8, 1989, when the weekend site manager went around to close the internal shutters. Coming to the rear bedroom, he found the room dark, the door closed, the lights off, and the shutters already bolted, when minutes earlier he had seen the door open and sunshine streaming through the windows. The exact incident repeated itself for another staff member 20 years later. (Courtesy of Merchant's House Museum.)

Other family members may account for some of the paranormal activities at the Merchant's House Museum. Like her younger sister Gertrude, Phebe Tredwell never married and lived her whole life in the house. In October 1907, she met her end in a painful way, falling down the stairs and breaking her neck and femur. Since her death, staff and visitors have experienced cold spots and oppressive energy surrounding the stairs. (Courtesy of Merchant's House Museum.)

The apparition of Seabury Tredwell's son Samuel appeared to a woman in 1999. As she peered at family photographs in an exhibition case, he appeared at her side, wearing a long overcoat smelling of mothballs. Indicating a hanging portrait, he said, "He built the house. I knew him very well." After he vanished, the staff showed her family portraits, and she identified the man as Samuel. (Courtesy of Merchant's House Museum.)

Other strange activities experienced at the Merchant's House Museum include the odors of cigar smoke, sweet violet toilet water, or toasted bread filling the air. Once, in the kitchen, a caretaker observed the 19th-century cast-iron stove shaking violently. Staff members also reported that the door to the kitchen swings open. On December 26, 2011, when a veteran tour guide walked the house, locking up, all of the servant bells in the kitchen rang furiously. When she stepped into the room, they stopped. Although the bell wires still existed, the pull strings for the bells had been removed. Other happenings such as the sound of children's footsteps, objects moving, the feeling of being poked or touched, the sensation of extreme heat, and one of the chandeliers swaying indicate that something is still at play in the house. (Courtesy of Merchant's House Museum.)

Phineas Taylor Barnum, the founder of the Ringling Bros. and Barnum & Bailey Circus, enjoyed many endeavors during his lifetime, including starting a newspaper, authoring several books, and running a statewide lottery. During his time in the Connecticut legislature, he spoke out against slavery. His lasting accomplishments were in the world of entertainment, where he established himself as an impresario when he introduced the beloved singer Jenny Linn to the American public.

In 1841, the self-professed showman purchased Scudder's American Museum, on the corner of Ann Street and Broadway, and turned it into one of the busiest attractions in New York City. For 25¢, visitors enjoyed historical dioramas; a wax museum; a zoo with monkeys, snakes, and an alligator; and even an aquarium with two live whales. Here, patrons also found shrunken heads, ancient mummies, and historical artifacts.

THE QUAKER GIANT AND GIANTESS
AS EXHIBITED AT BARNUMS AMERICAN MUSEUM, NEW YORK 1849.
The Giant is 8 feet high & weighs 308 Pounds. The Giantess is nearly 8 feet high & weighs 337 Pounds.

Phineas T. Barnum also became known for exhibiting people with unique physical characteristics. Measured at seven feet and eight inches tall, Englishman Robert Hales premiered at the American Museum as the Norfolk Giant. He later agreed to a pretend marriage to the seven-foot-two-inch-tall Eliza Simpson. They went on tour for two years as the Quaker Giants.

MISS SUSAN BARTON,
THE MAMMOTH LADY
as Exhibited at
BARNUM'S AMERICAN MUSEUM, NEW YORK 1869.
Weight 576 Pounds.

Other exhibits that amazed audiences included Miss Susan Barton, a 576-pound woman. She shared the spotlight with Zalumma Agra, the Star of the East, a beautiful woman with extraordinarily frizzy hair. Barnum claimed he rescued her from the slave markets of Constantinople. It was Barnum's ability to dazzle audiences that drew hundreds of visitors per hour. However, it all ended violently on July 13, 1865.

Shortly after 12:00 p.m., a fire broke out in a defective furnace in the cellar. Workers rushed to the second floor and broke the whale tanks, hoping the water would put out the fire. Instead, the whales were left to flounder and die in the heat. In the mad rush to escape, people knocked over the snake tanks. Boa constrictors and pythons slithered alongside escaping patrons. An enormous crowd gathered to watch the blaze, and when a steam fire engine shrieked in the distance, someone yelled, "The elephant is loose," causing mass panic. Despite numerous injuries, no humans died in the fire. However, all of the animals either perished in the flames or were killed by policemen. To this day, sensitive people continue to see apparitions of animals on the corner of Broadway and Ann Street. Some have even seen P.T. Barnum attempting to put out the flames. Since he did not die in the fire, it seems these ghosts may be emotional echoes destined to replay the horrific events of that terrible day.

Henry Clay Frick (left) amassed much wealth in the coke and steel industries. However, his actions as the chairman of Carnegie Steel garnered him critics and enemies. On July 23, 1892, anarchist Alexander Berkman, seen below in 1892, entered Frick's office and shot him. Two bullets that struck Frick in the neck did not kill him, and Frick said later that the ghost of his dead daughter Martha appeared and saved his life. Berkman said that his first shot missed Frick because bright sunlight shining in the window obscured his view; however, that seems unlikely, as the office window faced north and received no direct sunshine.

The former mansion of Henry Clay Frick, at 1 East Seventieth Street, houses the Frick Collection, which features paintings, sculpture, and art by Western artists. Frick's private art collection, as stipulated in his will at the time of his death, formed the foundation for the museum. Adjacent to the mansion is the Frick Art Reference Library, established in 1920 by Frick's daughter Helen. While the museum denies claims of any paranormal activities, stories have leaked out that Helen's presence watches over the museum and that the elevator has a habit of stopping without request on the second floor, where Helen and her parents' bedrooms were once located.

Born and raised in Manhattan, Washington Irving wrote satirical and historical essays, biographies, and short stories. Published in 1829, Irving's ghost story *The Legend of Sleepy Hollow* continues to be read today. Unlike the frightening ghost of the Headless Horseman he made famous, the ghost of Irving reportedly visits the places he held dear.

Upon his death in 1848, John Jacob Astor bequeathed money for a free public research library known as the Astor Library. The will also stipulated that Washington Irving was to be a trustee and the first chairman. In recent years, Irving's ghost has reportedly been seen in his home north of New York City on the Hudson River, but, after Irving's death in 1859, the Astor Library first marked his return.

Before Astor died, he made Joseph Green Cogswell (right) responsible for buying the books for the future library. Astor's will made Cogswell a trustee and the first librarian. Cogswell was a trusted friend to Washington Irving, so he immediately recognized Irving's specter when he came across it in the stacks months after Irving's death.

According to the diaries of George Templeton Strong (below), Irving was not the only ghost Cogswell saw at the library. On three occasions, a local attorney, Austin L. Sands, appeared to Cogswell, and, when asked why he was there, the phantom reportedly replied, "For variety." Templeton's diaries became better known for revealing insights into the public's opinions during the Civil War, and the Astor Library later became known as the Joseph Papp Public Theater.

JOSEPH GREEN COGSWELL
From a photograph probably taken about 1870

The Morgan Library (above), at 225 Madison Avenue, has an interesting relationship with ghosts. The institution came out of John Pierpont Morgan's love of collecting all forms of art, notably medieval manuscripts, rare books, and drawings. Morgan (left) began as an accountant and ended up heading one of the most powerful banking institutions in the world. His money and influence shaped railroads and emerging companies of that era such as General Electric and AT&T. A lover of art and books, Morgan contributed to the Metropolitan Museum of Art, and he built this library next to his home to house his many collections. The architect Charles F. McKim oversaw all of the design elements in the Renaissance-style building.

John Pierpont Morgan's study and library appear today much as they did in these two photographs from 1963. It is easy to imagine Morgan working with dealers or examining his Gutenberg Bible in these stately rooms. These furnishings may have inspired the library's first director, Belle da Costa Greene, to ask the literary author and historian Montague Rhodes James to write a ghost story for the museum, which he politely declined to do. This foiled request reemerged in a 1987 lecture given by staff member Hope Mayo, which inspired other museum staff to sponsor a ghost story contest with tales featuring the museum. Seven of the winning stories formed the basis of the book *Morgan Library Ghost Stories*. This collection was written so effectively that it could be mistaken for fact.

The Jefferson Market Courthouse, at Sixth Avenue and Tenth Street, replaced a public meat and produce market in 1877. The site included a jail and later a woman's detention center. In 1906, the arraignment of Harry K. Thaw for the murder of Stanford White took place there (see page 64). In 1967, the city converted the building into a public library, and the clock tower still chimes the hour today. One of the friendly librarians shared that some of her coworkers think the space may be haunted, as they have heard strange noises at closing time.

William M. Tweed rose from modest beginnings to lead the Tammany Hall Organization, a political engine in 19th-century New York. After serving a stint in the US House of Representatives, he returned to Manhattan to serve on the board of supervisors of New York County in 1858, and he became an active member of Tammany Hall in charge of the Seventh Ward, earning the nickname Boss. To ensure voter support, Tweed set up programs to aide the largely Catholic immigrant population and the poor. He used his political office for personal gain by establishing controlling interests in companies that the city hired for services and then charging inflated fees for those services rendered. Tweed Courthouse stands today as an impressive legacy of Tweed's corrupt business dealings. As president of the board of city supervisors in charge of the building's construction, he arranged the appropriation of $13 million to the project, much of which went into his own pocket.

A series of cartoons by Thomas Nash brought Boss Tweed's corrupt business dealings to the public's attention. The cartoon at left, published in *Harpers Weekly* on September 23, 1871, depicts Boss and his crew as buzzards waiting for a storm to pass to consume the scraps of New York City. These illustrations, coupled with a series of articles in the *New York Times*, led to his arrest in December 1871. After one trial ended in a hung jury, a second jury convicted him on 204 counts. Ironically, Boss Tweed stood trial and was sentenced in his own courthouse in 1873. The courthouse is seen below before it was renovated.

After one failed escape attempt, Tweed died in prison in 1878, and stories flourished about his haunting the instrument of his own fall, Tweed Courthouse. In 1911, a jury clerk, George F. Lyon, reported that he saw a figure walk across a courtroom one evening. He went on to say that court officer, Capt. William Rickets, saw Tweed in the closet of the courtroom where the Boss had stood trial. Additionally, two night watchmen were fired after refusing to enter the building at night, claiming to hear noises and see figures moving about the corridors. Contemporary accounts claim that the activity increases whenever political corruption is in the news.

CITY HALL, N.Y. CITY

Bodies lie beneath the ground surrounding New York City Hall, which may account for the paranormal activity that has been reported inside. The building, constructed from 1803 to 1812, was not the first institution located in the area known as the commons. Bridewell prison was to the west, and an almshouse was to the east. Many people who died from disease in these buildings, or by execution on the surrounding grounds, were buried in the park area. Some of those bodies were moved to the side grounds to make way for the present Beaux Arts–style building. Over the years, cleaning and security staffs have seen 19th-century apparitions in the basement area, and elevators have been known to malfunction at night.

106

H.R.Robinson 142 Nassau St. N.Y.   Pbr. D.T. Valentines   Hanna

THE OLD BRIDEWELL .

ch formerly stood in the Park, between the City Hall and Broadwa

On April 13, 1788, the Bridewell prison, on Broadway, became a sanctuary for some anatomy students. Once, little boys exploring the grounds of New York Hospital, located between Duane and Worth Streets on Broadway, discovered body parts in one room. Alarmed parents stormed the buildings and became enraged after finding a head boiling in a kettle and sex organs hanging on the wall. The parental mob realized the students had been robbing graves, and they began hunting for the culprits. Concerned for their safety, the mayor hid the budding physicians in the Bridewell, but the mob eventually learned the truth and stormed the grounds. The mayor formed a militia to defuse the crowd, but violence broke out between the factions, ending with five dead and eight injured. The students survived, but grave robbing became illegal.

By 1837, the Bridewell prison could no longer support Manhattan's criminal population, so the city built a larger institution on Centre Street, in the Five Points neighborhood. Designed after an Egyptian mausoleum, the prison became known as the Tombs. Many murderers met their end there, but John C. Colt's supposed suicide, hours before his execution, proved to be the most scandalous. Although his brother Samuel invented the Colt revolver, John used a hatchet to slay Samuel Adams, a printer he owed money to. After police discovered Adams's remains in a basket on a ship in September 1841, a sensational trial and guilty verdict quickly followed. John C. Colt faced execution on November 14, 1842. As the crowd grew outside for the public hanging, a fire broke out in the cupola of the Tombs prison. After the excitement, authorities discovered Colt in his cell, dead, stabbed in the heart. Perhaps because Colt had attempted to escape multiple times, stories arose that he had orchestrated a look-alike to die in his place and that he spent his remaining years living in California. Biographers have since discredited that idea.

The boggy land proved a poor foundation for the Tombs, and conditions grew damp, foul, and unsanitary. After public outcry grew about the deplorable situation, a new building was constructed on the same site in 1902 (right). The new prison featured a bridge connected to the criminal courts building, which became known as the Bridge of Sighs (below), because anyone crossing it lost their freedom and faced a depressing future. The swampy land underneath again produced dank, stinky conditions in the new jail, yet, despite its noxious reputation, some inhabitants received preferential treatment. Harry K. Thaw dined regularly from Delmonico's Restaurant and slept in a brass bed while awaiting his murder trail in 1906 (see page 64). When modern facilities replaced this building, it continued to be called the Tombs.

The old New York Times Building (above, second from right) is the last recognizable edifice from what was known as Newspaper Row. More than a dozen newspapers had their headquarters on Park Row until 1894, when they began moving uptown. Constructed in 1857 and enlarged in 1889, the old New York Times Building has long been thought haunted. The oldest story tells of an employee, Mary Wilson, coming to work many times in 1891 to find her desk in disarray. She thought her coworkers were to blame until she saw an apparition. In 1951, Pace University purchased the building, and the tales continued. In Pace's student newspaper, a former student wrote that she heard snoring as she was about to enter a lower-level lounge called the Billingbear Room. When she flipped on the light, the noise stopped, and she was startled to find the room empty. In her article, she wrote that legend has it that the college's founder, Homer Pace, haunts the building.

Five

SPIRITED TAVERNS
AND THEATERS

In 1880, longshoreman often gathered for a pint at the White Horse Tavern at Hudson and Eleventh Streets. In the 1950s, it attracted a literary crowd, and its most famous patron was Dylan Thomas. The poet liked his whisky and was a frequent visitor up until his death on November 9, 1953. When workers find his regular table unaccountably moved or hear noises in the cellar, they believe Thomas has paid a visit.

Mr. MACREADY
AS MACBETH.

Engraved by A.B.Durand from a painting by J.Neagle
Lopez & Wemyss' Edition
Published by Tho.° T. Ash. Philad.ª 1827
Copy Right secured according to Law

A performance of Shakespeare's *Macbeth* at the Astor Place Opera House on May 10, 1849, reignited the ancient struggle between the classes and became a vehicle for mayhem and the slaying of innocents. The characters in the real-life drama were both famous actors of the stage. When the events unfolded, the wealthy William Charles Macready, of London, had earned his fame after performing for 38 years in the best houses in England, Europe, and the United States.

In contrast, Edwin Forrest rose to stardom through lowbrow theaters in the western United States. When Forrest premiered in England, Macready welcomed the younger, greener actor. Forrest's second trip abroad set the fateful stage. After receiving poor reviews for his performance as Macbeth, Forrest claimed that Macready fueled the negative response, so he decided to attend Macready's performance of *Hamlet*, where he audibly hissed during the show, creating a firestorm of controversy.

GREAT RIOT AT THE ASTOR PLACE OPERA HOUSE, NEW YORK.
ON THURSDAY EVENING MAY 10TH 1849

When William Macready opened *Macbeth* at the Astor Place Opera House in New York on May 7, 1849, supporters of Edwin Forrest arranged for 500 audience members to disrupt the performance. The throwing of rotten eggs, various vegetables, and shoes stopped the show. Society's elite, led by Washington Irving, pronounced their support of Macready and convinced him to perform again. When city officials expressed their concern, theater promoters pressed their legal claim and demanded support. Three days later, on May 10, when Macready stepped on the stage, he met hissing and cheers. This time, the police arrested hostile spectators. In the street, more than 10,000 people gathered to watch a small, volatile group rail against the upper classes. Young men hurled rocks into the windows of the theater. When some tried to set it on fire, the military arrived, causing the rioters to turn violent. After 50 troops sustained injuries, the order was given to fire. The death toll numbered 23, mostly innocent bystanders. Macready, in disguise, escaped the theater unharmed.

Before the Metropolitan Opera moved to its new home in Lincoln Center in 1966, it occupied this 3,700-seat Italian Renaissance building located at Broadway and Thirty-ninth Street. Families of the nouveau riche, including the Morgans, Goulds, and Roosevelts, drove the formation of the new opera company in 1883, after they were denied box seats at the long-established Academy of Music. The Met flourished, with the greatest stars, like Enrico Caruso, playing there.

Soprano Frances Alda performed with the Met for 29 years, often singing opposite Caruso. After her death in 1952, her ghost reportedly returned to annoy people. Appearing in silk and pearls, she would occupy an orchestra seat and grouse about the poor singing by the sopranos. In 1955, one patron complained to an usher about the distracting woman, only to be told by fellow guests that the seat had been empty the entire performance.

For a ballet to succeed, the musicians and dancers who come together must trust each other implicitly. It is in that safe environment that an artist will achieve greatness through being vulnerable. On July 23, 1980, a stagehand at the Metropolitan Opera in Lincoln Center shattered that trust, murdering a 30-year-old violinist during a performance by the Berlin Ballet. The former Julliard graduate left her violin on her seat during intermission and encountered her killer in an elevator; he then bound her and dragged her to the roof. After fighting off an attempted assault, the woman was hurled off the roof down an airshaft to her death. A jury convicted the 21-year-old stagehand, Craig S. Crimmins, and the judge sentenced him to 20 years to life. All of Crimmins's petitions for parole, beginning in 2001, have been denied. At the time of this writing, his last hearing occurred on May 15, 2012.

Florence Ziegfeld, known as Flo to his friends, made his fortune as a theatrical impresario. Unfortunately, he lost much of it in the stock market crash of 1929, and he died deeply in debt in 1932. In 1907, he launched the Ziegfeld Follies, and the show's popularity lasted until 1931. The revue-like format brought together vaudeville talent like Fanny Brice, Eddie Cantor, Josephine Baker, and W.C. Fields; music from top composers such as Irving Berlin; and elaborately staged scenes with beautiful women. Some of the Ziegfeld girls entertained audiences in a more risqué program called the Midnight Frolic (below), which was held in the rooftop garden of the New Amsterdam Theatre after the regular show. This invitation-only venue featured a glass balcony where the men below could gaze up the skirts of the showgirls parading above them.

One ghost story linked to the Ziegfeld Follies involves the tragic death of Ziegfeld girl Olive Thomas. Ziegfeld learned of Thomas after she won the Most Beautiful Girl in New York City contest. In September 1920, while vacationing in France with her husband, Jack Pickford, she died from devastating complications after ingesting bio-chloride. Rumors swirled that Pickford murdered her for her money, or that she committed suicide due to a failed affair with Ziegfeld, but Paris police ruled her death an accident. Built in 1903, the New Amsterdam Theatre (the tallest building at right) housed the performances from 1913 to 1927, and it is where Thomas appeared to stagehands shortly after her death. Just months before the theater's April 2, 1995, reopening, after Disney spent $34 million to restore it, Thomas reportedly startled a night watchman. Thomas's ghost still seems very active, but she appears only to men.

The ghost of David Belasco reportedly still visits the Belasco Theatre on West Forty-fifth Street. A successful impresario, director, and playwright, Belasco revolutionized lighting and set design. Collections from his vast library launched Lincoln Center's Library of the Performing Arts. Although he was born Jewish, Belasco earned the name the Bishop of Broadway by dressing like a priest, in all black with a white collar. He spent many hours in his office and his 10-room apartment above the theater, where, like in the *Phantom of the Opera*, he had numerous spy holes, allowing him to see all aspects of the theater below. Since his death in 1931, stagehands have heard the long-dead mechanisms for his personal elevator come to life, as though taking him up to his apartment, where party noises can still be heard.

Although he was married, Belasco had a reputation with the ladies—he is seen here with Vera Bloom in 1923—and his ghost continues to pinch the backsides of chorus girls. He also announces his presence in other ways. One evening, when the last usher to leave said, "Goodnight, Mr. Belasco," the lobby doors swung wide open. The usher never returned. Stagehands have heard footsteps late at night and smelled his cigar, and many have reported seeing him sitting in his former seat during rehearsals and on opening nights of shows. A cast member from the 2004 production of *Dracula* said he exchanged a few words with a man fitting Belasco's description. However, Belasco is not there alone. Another apparition called the Blue Lady has been seen in the balcony, leaving a cool draft in her wake.

Opening in 1913, the Palace, the tall building in the center, became a premier vaudeville theater. After a stint as a movie house, the theater reclaimed its glory in the 1950s, when it hosted stellar performances by Frank Sinatra and Judy Garland. However, some acts have refused to leave. On August 27, 1935, Louis Bossalina fell 18 feet to the stage while performing with an acrobatic team, the Four Casting Pearls. Although he recovered from his substantial injuries and lived until 1963, stagehands have reported seeing his ghost swinging from the dress circle rim and hearing him yell as he falls. Other ghosts include a sad little girl who looks down from the mezzanine and a man in a brown suit who walks past the manager's office at night. An actor in the 1995 production of *Beauty and the Beast* reported seeing a white-gowned cellist in the orchestra pit vanish. Intrigued cast members asked a psychic to do a reading on October 6, 1995, and she reported that many spirits still clamor for the audience's attention.

Musical theater's best-known choreographer, Bob Fosse, began by performing on Broadway and in movie musicals. He turned to choreography with *The Pajama Game*, earning the first of an unprecedented eight Tony awards for choreography. Because of pressure from producers to remove the sexual expression from his numbers, the inventor of "jazz hands" turned to directing, winning an Academy Award for the movie *Cabaret*, which beat out Francis Ford Coppola's *The Godfather*. He died at age 60 in Washington, DC, but still returns to the 46th Street Theatre, which was later renamed the Richard Rogers Theatre. He worked there multiple times, including for the show at left. He was a chain-smoker and he always wore hats. Since his death, hats have suddenly appeared in the theater, and when cold spots crop up or the smell of tobacco smoke fills the air, everyone knows Fosse is in the house.

Despite the start of the Great Depression of 1929, John D. Rockefeller Jr. proceeded with plans to build a commercial complex of buildings north of the notorious Tenderloin district. With RKO Studios as a partner, he brought together the design talents of architect Edward Durell Stone, interior designer Donald Deskey, and impresario Samuel "Roxy" Rothafel (below) to create a magnificent theater as the center point. Eventually named Radio City Music Hall, its 5,874 seats made it the largest indoor theater in the world at the time. Deskey's Art Deco interior still draws rave reviews; it features 30 uniquely designed spaces, incorporating murals and fine art elements. Rothafel's ghost is said to still linger in the great space.

Rothafel came to Rockefeller's attention because of his radio show, which was broadcast from inside the Capitol Theater and had five million listeners, and because he successfully blended live entertainment with movies. At Radio City, he added a dance troupe, originally called the Missouri Rockets and known today as the Rockettes, to the showing of popular motion pictures. Rothafel did not enjoy his magnificent showplace for long, as he died in 1936, just four years after it opened. Sometimes, after ushers have put up all the seats at night, they have found Roxy's seat down, as though he had been there peering over the mezzanine. Other stories tell of his ghost being seen walking to his seat with a stunning woman on his arm. His presence has also been felt in his still-maintained private apartment, located inside the theater.

In 1924, the Providence Players turned a box factory into the longest operating off-Broadway venue, the Cherry Lane Theatre. Experimental theater movements and the works of notable playwrights such as Eugene O'Neill, Sean O'Casey, Clifford Odets, Samuel Beckett, Pablo Picasso, Tennessee Williams (left), Harold Pinter, Edward Albee, Sam Shepard, and David Mamet came from this humble space. Exceptional performers like Betty Davis, Barbara Streisand, James Earl Jones, Harvey Keitel, Gene Hackman, and F. Murray Abraham have trod its boards. The apparitions of two men reportedly join them. The ghosts appear so indistinct that no one knows who they are. White mist forms the shape of one man near the lobby stairs, while the other appears as a dark shadow near the dressing rooms. Cold spots accompany their visitations, and cast and crew have also heard unaccountable noises.

The Delancy family home, built in 1719, became the Fraunces Tavern in 1762. The building's design was altered after a fire in 1832 and again in 1890, when a storefront with additional floors was added (above). The city prevented its demolition and turned it over to the Sons of the Revolution, who restored it to its original Colonial design in 1907 (below). Sometimes, paranormal activity seems to arise not because of a human spirit, but instead from human emotions. Residual hauntings can occur after dramatic events that trigger strong emotional responses. This energy can then become a part of the fabric of the space, and when sensitive people pass through that environment's ether, they experience the past. At the Fraunces Tavern, people claim to have heard the clink of glasses, the scrapping of chairs, and the murmur of voices in the Long Room on the tavern's second floor.

In Fraunces Tavern's Long Room on December 4, 1783, George Washington bid an emotional farewell to his executive officers. It had been a hard-fought conflict, and they had suffered great trials together. When Washington stood to make his farewell speech, his voice quaked, his hands shook, and his eyes filled with tears. After he had finished, he asked the men to come to him, as he feared his legs would not carry him across the floor. Stepping into that room today, the past whispers to the living like a ghost, whether real or imagined. Washington's words, spoken then in earnest, remain a stirring sentiment to those who read them now: "With a heart full of love and gratitude, I now take leave of you. I most devoutly wish that your latter days may be as prosperous and happy as your former ones have been glorious and honorable." (From the original manuscript, *The Memoir of Col. Benjamin Tallmadge*, page 103. Courtesy of the collection of the Fraunces Tavern Museum.)

BIBLIOGRAPHY

Bellov, Anthony. *Some Say They Never Left*. New York City: Merchant's House Museum, 2007.

Blackhall, Susan. *Ghosts of New York*. San Diego, CA: Thunder Bay Press, 2005.

Dash, Mike. *Satan's Circus: Murder, Vice, Police Corruption, and New York's Trial of the Century*. New York City: Three Rivers Press, 2007.

Ferrara, Eric. *A Guide to Gangsters, Murderers, and Weirdos of New York City's Lower East Side*. Charleston, SC: The History Press, 2009.

Hladik, L'Aura. *Ghosthunting New York City*. Cincinnati, OH: Clerisy Press, 2010.

Jackson, Kenneth T., ed. *The Encyclopedia of New York City*. New Haven, CT: Yale University, 1995.

Lanigan-Schmidt, Therese. *Ghosts of New York City*. Atglen, PA: Schiffer Publishing Ltd., 2003.

Macken, Lynda Lee. *Ghostly Gotham: New York City's Haunted History*. Forked River, NJ: Black Cat Press, 2002.

Schoenberg, Dr. Philip Ernest. *Ghosts of Manhattan*. Charleston, SC: The History Press, 2009.

Stein, Leon. *The Triangle Fire*. Centennial Edition. Ithaca, NY: Cornell University Press, 2011.

Von Pressentin Wright, Carol, Stuart Miller, and Sharon Seitz. *New York Blue Guide*. London, England: A&C Black Publishers, 2002.

Willis, Clint, ed. *Crimes of New York: Stories of Crooks, Killers, and Corruption from the World's Toughest City*. New York City: Thunder's Mouth Press, 2003.

DISCOVER THOUSANDS OF LOCAL HISTORY BOOKS FEATURING MILLIONS OF VINTAGE IMAGES

Arcadia Publishing, the leading local history publisher in the United States, is committed to making history accessible and meaningful through publishing books that celebrate and preserve the heritage of America's people and places.

Find more books like this at
www.arcadiapublishing.com

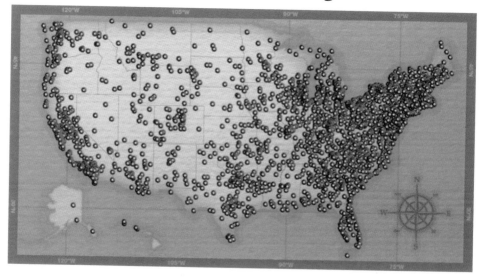

Search for your hometown history, your old stomping grounds, and even your favorite sports team.